365
Ways to
BUILD
YOUR CHILD'S
SELF-ESTEEM

CHERI FULLER

PIÑON PRESS

P.O. Box 35007, Colorado Springs, Colorado 80935

Library of Congress Catalog Card Number:
    94-67031
ISBN 08910-98550

Cover illustration: Bob Fuller

Printed in the United States of America

Published in association with the literary
agency of Alive Communications, P.O. Box
    49068, Colorado Springs, CO 80949.

To Alison Delaine Fuller

A Note to Parents

Self-esteem: Children need it; the stresses, changes, and cruelties of life batter it. One study showed that the average child hears over 10,000 negative messages about himself before he graduates from high school like, "You're stupid. Shut up. You nerd." How can we as parents be part of the building up rather than the tearing down of our children's self-worth?

We know self-esteem is the foundation of motivation, mental development, and healthy relationships. A child with a positive self-image is able to concentrate on school work, try new activities, make friends, and weather the stresses and changes of life. He feels capable and is willing and able to take responsibility. He learns to verbalize instead of stuff his anger. Making wise decisions, resisting peer pressure, making the most of his intellect and skills—the young person who feels he has worth is more successful at all of these important tasks.

In contrast, a child with low self-esteem

tends to have trouble in school, difficulty getting along with teachers and making friends, and is at-risk for substance abuse and repeated failures in the classroom and job market.

A secure, trusting parent-child relationship is the cornerstone of a child's sense of self-worth. By the end of the first year of life, children have begun developing a mental picture of who they are, and that picture continues developing through childhood. And in all the daily routines, rituals, and activities of family life, we have a myriad of opportunities to nurture our children's self-esteem. As we fill their cups with encouragement, love, acceptance, affection, and understanding, they grow up knowing they are cherished and respected. Then as our children meet obstacles and challenges (and even fail, at times) they get encouragement and positive feedback and gain the momentum to try again.

This book is full of 365 ways to build your child's self-esteem. Not with an empty, over-inflated conceit, but a self-worth filled with real substance: learning how to work hard to achieve in school, how to help and contribute at home, how to support and appreciate other people, be a friend, and use his strengths and talents. Not a false self-esteem, but one based on growing skills. It's also packed with creative ideas to show your love and affection for your child and to keep open the lines of communication throughout childhood and adolescence.

I hope you and your child enjoy all 365 ways!

1

When your son or daughter goes to camp,
write small notes for every day,
labeled "Day 1," "Day 2,"
etc., and hide them in his or her suitcase
with encouraging words like,
"Make a new friend today! Love you,
Mom." "I'm thinking of you today. Have
a great time swimming. See you Saturday."

2

"When someone is deprived
of his self-esteem,
he is deprived of the one thing
that makes him feel worth loving."
—JO COUDERT

3

Sing to your baby. Listen to music,
and sing together as a family,
each child keeping the rhythm
with a simple instrument.

4

Save your child's best schoolwork
in a manila file folder labeled
with her name, the date, and age.
Take the files out and peruse them
occasionally so your child
can see the strides she's made in drawing,
handwriting, math, and other skills.

5

Write a note to your child
with encouraging words like,
"Nice job reorganizing your room!"
or "I love you. Let's play catch after
school." Tuck it in his lunch bag or box.

6

Avoid labels like "clumsy," "motor mouth,"
or other negatives.
Children often become what their parents
and teachers expect them to be.

As many evenings as you can,
put a centerpiece
on your table—a vase of flowers,
some apples, or decorated eggs
in a basket—light candles,
and express thanks
for your children
(and something specific about each one)
and that you are a family.

Set guidelines that build a sense
of family unity, such as,
"In our family we don't hurt
each other with harsh words;
instead we build each other up,"
or "In our family we keep our
commitments,
and we start things we finish."

9

Focus on the donut instead of the hole:
the eighty points she got right on the test,
the one basket she made in the game
instead of the four she missed,
the positive instead of the negative
things she is doing.

10

On your family bulletin board
or refrigerator tack inspirational,
positive sayings you find, such as, "You
can't steal second with your foot on first,"
or "Don't give up. Keep going.
There is always a chance that you will
stumble onto something terrific!"

11

Keep a record of the positive
comments and encouraging words
you give your child during one day.
Try increasing the number the next day.

12

Write a letter to put in your child's
Christmas stocking each year
that expresses appreciation
for the person he is,
for the growth and progress
he's had during the year,
and the combination of mental,
social, spiritual, and physical
qualities you are thankful for.

13

Give your child daily,
age-appropriate chores at home
that help the family
and build her sense of being
capable and responsible.

14

Show interest and listen to your child's
problems, big and small.

15

Go to your child's sports events,
parents' day at school, drama or music
presentations, and awards ceremonies.

———◆———

16

Set clear, specific limits for behavior
in your home.

———◆———

17

Major on the majors,
keeping rules to a minimum but enforcing
consistently those you establish
in your family.

———◆———

18

Have a regular routine at your home
for eating, doing chores, sleeping,
studying, and spending time together.

19

Holding your child often,
patting his shoulder,
holding his hand when you walk,
builds a sense of inner security.
(In adolescence,
the hand-holding may have to go,
but young children appreciate it.)

20

Be a positive role model.
What you do in your life,
modeling the behavior you
hope to see in your child,
is more important than the rules
you set or what you say,
because children learn
best by imitation.

21

Help your child become an "expert"
on something (knowing more on a topic
of interest to her than anyone
in the family or even her classroom).

22

Have great expectations for your child.
Children tend to live up—or down—
to their reputation and our expectations.

23

Regularly play a game of Ping Pong
or a board game with your child and keep
track of the score from round to round.

24

Help your child understand
that actions and decisions have
consequences for himself and others.

25

Be available to your child
on a regular basis so that she knows
she can count on you for focused
attention when she needs
a listening ear
or help with a problem.

26

Instead of finishing your child's
sentences or answering for him
when someone has asked him a question,
be patient and give
him a chance to respond.

27

Create an environment at home where
your children can feel safe
in communicating anything to you
without fear of criticism or overreaction.

28

Visit your child's classroom at school,
either by bringing cookies for a party
or helping out with a project.
Learn about what she does
at school and what she likes
to learn about the most.

29

When a problem crops up at school,
think the best instead of the worst of your
child, and hear his side of the situation
before forming any conclusions.

30

Smile at your child frequently.
Kids see themselves in the mirror
we hold up to them in our looks
of approval or disapproval.

31

Have lunch with your child
once a month in the school cafeteria.

32

Encourage your child
to be friendly by showing her
how a handshake, a kind word,
or a warm smile helps build
relationships with others.

33

Show your child how to ask
for advice or help on a subject
or assignment from the reference
librarian or teacher,
and encourage him
to approach the person
when assistance is needed.

34

Help your child see that she has
many unique God-given attributes,
things to contribute in a class or group,
and traits that will attract people
when she is herself.

35

Encourage your child to keep
his negative thoughts and imaginings
about what might happen
to a minimum, and not worry
or exaggerate circumstances.

36

Help your child keep physically fit
with regular times for outdoor play,
sports, swimming, and walking.

37

In addition to school opportunities,
continually challenge your child's
mind to grow by learning new things:
taking a summer computer course,
taking cooking lessons,
checking out and reading books
on a totally new subject.

38

Encourage your child
to keep mistakes in perspective
(we all make them,
and in fact,
many successful people fail
on their way to success),
overcome setbacks,
and even enjoy the trial-and-error
process of learning.

39

Help your child learn
to concentrate
and focus on one task or activity
at a time by assembling a puzzle,
playing a game,
or working on
and finishing a craft together—
completing the task before going on
to something else.

40

Give your child her own "space"
in your home, even if only a corner
of a room shared with a sibling,
to put up mementoes
on her bulletin board,
decorate the wall in her favorite way,
and make decisions
on how to organize and keep the space.

41

Teach your child manners,
like saying "please" and "thank you,"
insist on his using them,
and set an example by using
good manners yourself.

42

Never do a task or assignment
for your child that she could
do for herself.

43

Pitch a tent in your back yard,
and let your child
"camp" there overnight
with a sibling or friend.

44

Take your child's feelings
and ideas seriously.
Don't belittle him
with statements like,
"You'll grow out of it"
or "It's not nearly as bad
as you think."

45

Set aside time before bed
for listening, reading, or visiting
about your child's day,
giving her your undivided attention,
without scolding or seeking to improve
her behavior or performance in any way.

46

Use the imperfect, lumpy clay vase
your child created in art class for flowers
from your garden.

47

Have pencils engraved with your child's
name for the beginning of school.

48

Serve breakfast in bed on your child's
birthday, with a balloon attached
to the tray and his favorite
breakfast cereal.

49

When your child is sick in bed,
show kindness by: ▶ giving your child
some "TLC" time, playing a quiet game
or reading a book aloud; ▶ serving meals
on a colorful tray with a flower or treat;
▶ making sure it's not too soon
to be sent back to school.

50

Have realistic, in-reach expectations
for your child. You shouldn't expect
her to be the winner in every activity
she tries or expect a two-year-old
to act like a ten-year-old.

51

Accept your child's strengths
and weaknesses, flaws
and assets so he can learn
to accept himself.

52

Instead of comparing
your child to others
or reminding her she's just like Aunt Judy,
help your child see that she's
a one-of-a-kind person.

53

Children need daily praise to develop
into healthy individuals,
but make sure to give genuine compliments
when he does well or improves,
makes a wise decision,
or puts out extra effort.
Flattery falls flat,
while sincere praise encourages.

54

Pay as much attention to your child
when she talks to you
as when an adult you respect talks to you.

55

"No one, great or obscure,
is untouched by genuine appreciation.
We have a double necessity:
to be commended
and to know how to commend."
—FULTON OURSLER

56

Write a list
of what you're grateful for
about your child.
Add to it when
you discover new positive qualities
and strengths,
and jot down ways
to develop and use
his skills constructively.

57

Help your child or teen
tape record her own oral history.
Be the interviewer
and ask questions about
her earliest memory,
first home,
first "scars,"
camp experiences,
friends, adventures, etc.

58

"Praising a child does not spoil
the child. It is the child who does not
receive praise for worthy work
when he deserves it who will
seek praise in bizarre ways.
So when the gang praises him for cheating
or stealing he will naturally seek
to become an expert at that."
—JOHN M. DRESHER

59

Fall in love with your child
every day all over again
just because of who she is.

60

Let your child name the new kitten,
puppy, or gerbil.

61

If we focus on children's failures,
unpleasant behavior, and what they didn't
accomplish, they lose confidence;
but if we point out their improvement,
they gain the momentum to try harder.

62

Get down (or up!) on his level,
giving your child attention
and looking into his eyes
when he talks to you.

63

Make a colorful sign that says,
"YOU CAN DO IT!" or "GO FOR IT.
WE'RE BEHIND YOU!" to show your support
for a sports or music tryout
your child is in.

64

Make time at dinner to talk
about what your child is learning
at school, what activities are coming up,
and what concerns she has.

65

Offer your services to aid
your child in rearranging his furniture
in his bedroom or reorganizing
his closet or toys.

66

Keep a sense of humor;
look at everyday situations
(and your own foibles) in a lighthearted
way instead of deadly serious,
and help your child to do the same.
Look for the humorous comic strip
to share, watch a comedy movie,
and have fun together.

67

When your child has made a mistake,
instead of saying, "I told you so,"
or "You goofed again," try asking,
"What do you think you can
learn from this?"

———◆———

68

Have your child's name imprinted
on her favorite color of stationery, add
stamps and envelopes in a basket,
and encourage her to write to a friend
who has moved or a relative who will keep
up a regular correspondence.

———◆———

69

Frame and hang
your child's best art in a special,
visible place in your home.

70

Suggest that your child invite a friend over
and plan a snack ahead of time to offer.

71

When both parents stick together to agree
upon and enforce the family guidelines
and rules, children develop into healthier,
more confident young people.

72

"To err is human."
Don't expect perfection from your child.

73

Allow your child to have his own place
and time for privacy that is respected
by each member of the family;
have a "knock before entering" bedroom
rule. We all need to be alone
and have some quiet at times.

74

Participate in holiday family traditions
that build a sense of belonging
and create happy memories,
such as decorating the tree together,
helping someone less fortunate,
making cookies,
and creating thoughtful gifts
for each other.

75

Help your child open a savings account
at the bank and start saving
for a future goal of her choice.

76

Make it a goal to eat at least one
meal a day together, as a family,
with the television off,
phone unplugged,
and conversation the centerpiece.

77

Build a sense of teamwork
and cooperation by tackling big
household jobs together,
such as cleaning the garage
or raking all the leaves.
Then go out for ice cream
to celebrate the completion of the task.

78

Designate a basket or box
the "Thankful Place,"
and in the month of November,
write notes of appreciation for blessings,
nice things a family member does,
and positive character qualities
to put in the basket.
On Thanksgiving Day,
take turns at the table
reading these praise
and encouragement notes.

79

Put positive mottoes up
in your child's room and he can
learn them by heart, like,
"If at first you don't succeed, try, try
again!" "Dream the impossible dream!"
or "God doesn't make junk."

80

To spare your child embarrassment,
correct her in private
instead of in front of her friends.

81

Get out your family photo
albums and your child's
baby books and tell him how you
prepared and looked forward
to his arrival, the day of his birth
or adoption, and some highlights
of his first year.

82

Find something you
and your child can both enjoy doing
together—whether that is painting,
collecting rocks, kicking the football,
or making a model.

83

Get or make a plate that says
"You are special today" and celebrate your
child's learning to ride her bike,
making the team, or achieving a good
grade on the spelling test.

84

Take your child out for a meal
and conversation—just the two of you—
once or twice each month.

85

Talk with your child
and write down the short-term
and long-term goals she wants
to work on this month.
(*Examples:* read two books a week,
learn to make and serve
a complete meal, etc.)

86

Celebrate your child's special "firsts":
first lost tooth, first day of school
or summer vacation, first recital,
first Scouting badge, or first school award.

87

Enroll your child in a course
at the community center or YMCA
in a special interest or skill he wants
to learn: calligraphy, tumbling, art,
drama, martial arts, or dance.

88

Teach your child to complete work
before playing.

89

Use a variety of positive expressions
like "our family artist,"
"our map-reader and navigator,"
or "the family historian."

90

Don't rush to answer
all your child's questions.
Help her discover the answers
by looking up the information,
checking a dictionary or library,
or thinking through the dilemma
and brainstorming
for possibilities.

91

When you make a mistake
that hurts your child, admit it, apologize,
and ask his forgiveness,
so he can learn how to forgive those who
offend him and how to admit his
wrongdoing and ask forgiveness.

92

When you review your child's school
papers weekly or nightly, mention
something specific like, "That math drill
you've been doing
each afternoon is helping!"

93

To encourage communication,
discuss your own struggles,
disappointments, and successes
that you had as a young person
and how you overcame them.

94

Pray with your child at night
about her fears, problems,
and challenges in the near future.

95

When you teach your child
to do household jobs:
break the chore down into steps;
provide the needed supplies;
and demonstrate the correct method
to do the task.

96

Teach your child how to negotiate
with others, solve conflicts,
and get along with friends and siblings.

97

Use yellow sticky notes to write
reminders, "Hi Chris, I know you are busy
with school and sports,
but don't forget to feed
the dog—Love, Mom,"
or "Pick up Legos after you and Carl
play—Thanks, Dad,"
instead of nagging, yelling,
or letting frustration build.

98

Instead of fixing or changing
your child's essays and stories
written for school,
have her read her writing aloud
and after pointing out something good,
talk about ways to improve it.

99

Love can't be expressed
without making time
for the person we love.
To kids, love is spelled T-I-M-E.

———◆———

100

Give your child a sense of family
heritage and belonging by helping him
interview an older relative
and record on audio or videotape
some of the family's history.

———◆———

101

Have your child write
and send thank you notes
to people who have done something
helpful or nice for her,
and compliment at least
two things about the person
in the note.

102

Let your child know you believe in him
100 percent, that you are behind
him to support him in doing his very best.

103

Take your child to work with you
some day so she can see what you do
and meet your coworkers.

104

Give your child "heroes,"
people from the past or present
he can look up to who had courage,
overcame obstacles, and made a positive
impact on society. Books, movies,
and newspapers are good places
to introduce these heroes
to your child—like astronaut Sally Ride,
Red Cross founder Clara Barton, Civil War
President Abraham Lincoln.

105

Share your values with your child
and describe the experiences in your life
that helped determine your convictions
and the decisions you made
to accept certain beliefs.

106

Before your child comes home
from camp or a weekend away,
make a "WELCOME HOME!" poster
with bright markers
to put on the front door.

107

"Treat your child as a person of worth,
like 'company.'"
—JOHN DRESCHER

108

Give your child chances
to practice making decisions:
choosing the place for the Saturday family
outing or dividing the chores up
fairly and writing them down
for each person.

109

Provide a personal diary or journal
for your child to record her own stories,
memories, hopes, adventures,
and travel experiences.

110

Don't protect your child
from all consequences.
Sometimes kids need to learn
the painful way, experiencing the results
of their actions.

111

When your child learns
that he can talk to you
and won't be ignored or ridiculed,
he feels safe in expressing worries
and doubts that he would otherwise
keep to himself.

———◆———

112

Avoid comparing your child
to another—inside or outside
the family—by saying,
"Why can't you make A's
like your sister?"
or "Why don't you behave
like your friend Susan?"
Your child needs to know
she is accepted and loved
simply because she is herself.

113

Help your child learn what
his real talents are
by giving him opportunities
to experience many activities and find out
what he likes to do and is good at.

114

Don't hover over your child.
Assume she is competent and can handle
things, and your actions will
communicate your confidence in her.

115

Be spontaneous and fun. Break into song
and share a silly joke now and then
with your child.

116

Instead of blaming or verbally
attacking when your child
makes a mistake
("Why do you always make a mess?"),
help your child focus on what
has occurred and what needs to be
done to remedy the situation:
"I see the garage floor
has paint spilled on it.
You'll need to get
a sponge and some paint remover,
and clean it up."

117

Tell your child what behavior you
do want instead of what you don't want:
"The couch is for sitting," or
"We need to use quiet indoor voices
in the library."

118

Encourage your child to do
work outside your home
in the neighborhood to teach
responsibility and independence,
such as dogsitting
for a vacationing
neighbor, weeding gardens,
or babysitting.
He can make a colorful flyer
advertising his services
and distribute it.

119

Make a fun trip out of back-to-school
shopping. Even if your child needs
only a backpack and athletic shoes,
stop for a soda,
chat about the upcoming
school year, and enjoy
the time together.

120

Take your child on an "occupational"
field trip in your community.
There are a world of vocations to visit,
depending on your child's interests:
computer specialists, engineers,
nurses, emergency services, judges,
artists, professors. . . .

121

"The real job in education
comes long before children get to school.
You've got to have kids
feeling good about themselves,
feeling self-confident and ready to learn."

—DR. TERRY BRAZELTON

122

Use positive words that communicate
your appreciation—"You mean the world
to me," "You're a joy!" "You made my day."

123

Hold your child to academic
standards that are reasonable but high,
and support your child's reaching those
goals by teaching her how to set aside
time to study and showing her study
strategies that help her achieve.

124

Instead of calling your child "good"
or "bad," or assigning any label,
describe the behavior he is exhibiting:
"Your tracking mud into the kitchen has
to stop," or "The fighting you two are doing
is unpleasant and needs to stop."

125

Give your child permission to fail.
Help her see mistakes and failures
as building blocks that help us improve
and do better the next time around.

126

Help your child develop dreams
and goals he wants to reach,
places he wants to go,
things he wants to do someday.
Listen even to the big dreams,
brainstorm about steps to meet the goals,
and assure your child that he
can do whatever he's willing
to work for and persevere at.

127

Develop your child's creativity
and imagination by reading to her
from classic literature,
encouraging role-playing,
and taking her
to theater productions.

128

Have a "Family Talent Night"
once a month in which
each member of the family
gets up in front of the others
and sings a song,
demonstrates a new Karate move,
plays a composition
on his instrument,
recites a poem.
Only positive feedback,
applause, and enjoyment are displayed
after each "performance."

129

Help your child develop
language skills by talking
and listening a lot at home,
reading books aloud, and capitalizing
on dinner table conversation
to develop speaking skills.

130

Show your child how to nurture
relationships with friends—to put
out the effort to be caring,
to rejoice when something good
happens to her friend (perhaps writing
a note of congratulations),
to hold secrets in confidence,
to be thoughtful on birthdays.

131

Find out what your child
does well and find opportunities
for him to do more of it—whether that is
kicking a soccer ball, drawing, selling,
or serving others in need.

132

Emphasize what your child is learning
both in and out of the classroom,
rather than just standardized test scores
and report card grades.

133

Provide support and structure
for your child to succeed
in the classroom by helping her organize
her studies and materials.

———◆———

134

Help your child balance
scheduled activities like lessons
and team practices with time
for unstructured play,
rest, and reflection.

———◆———

135

Try replacing negatives like
won't, can't, and *that's wrong*
with words like *you can do it,
you're improving,
let's look at the problem.*

136

Avoid giving overblown, profuse praise
for things your child does.
("You are fabulous. You'll be an Olympic
gold medal winner.
You'll be a star on Broadway.")
Although praise is needed
to recognize the accomplishments
a child has worked for,
constant extravagant praise can
produce conceit or fear of failure.

137

Teach your child to give recognition
to others for a job well done and for help
he's received. Model for him
how to give a compliment.

138

Help your child stop wasting time
remediating all her weaknesses
and instead exercise her strengths.

139

Let your child know
you are eager to hear his ideas
and opinions about things:
current events, friends,
books, and issues.

140

Be your child's cheerleader:
Applaud her efforts and celebrate
the steps along the way to success.

141

Individual activities—tennis,
playing the drums, jogging,
or swimming—are often better than
competitive teams, especially for kids
with perfectionist tendencies.

142

Encourage your child to build a collection
of something that interests him:
rocks, baseball cards, shells, or coins,
and supply a special shelf
or clear plastic organizer to keep
and display the collection.

143

Help your child discover whether
she learns best by seeing and reading
about things (visual),
and talking about a subject (auditory),
or touching and moving
while learning (kinesthetic),
and then use that strength
to study and learn.

144

If your child seems to be a "late bloomer,"
be confident that he will bloom when
the child and the timing are right.

145

Remind your child
that success in any area comes from
hard work, *practice*, and *perseverance*,
but that you will be supporting her
along the way.

———◆———

146

"Love forgets mistakes;
nagging about them parts
the best of friends."
—KENNETH TAYLOR

———◆———

147

Fly a kite, throw a baseball,
or walk around the block
with your child to allow time
for openness and hearing his concerns.
It's easier for him to express feelings
and thoughts when "heated up"
and engaged in activity.

148

Hug your child when she is
the most unlovable, the most "prickly"
and negative.

———◆———

149

When your child is afraid,
he needs to be listened to
and loved. Communicate to him
that his fears are real
and that together you can
come up with solutions and ways
to deal with them.

———◆———

150

Praise your child for wise choices
she makes about using her time,
completing homework and chores,
or handling problems.

151

Watch for the skills your child
catches on to and learns rapidly—these are
areas of strength to develop and tap into.

152

Assist your child in problem solving.
When a decision is to be made,
together you can write a pro-con list,
weigh the alternatives and possible
consequences, and help him arrive
at a decision or solution to the problem.

153

Write a note of encouragement
to your child—it doesn't have to be long,
just something sincere and specific
you see your child doing
or improving on that you appreciate.
Tuck it under her bedroom door
or tape it to her mirror.

154

Find out what your child enjoys
and finds real satisfaction in learning
about and look for ways
he can find out more.

155

Sow seeds of self-confidence
in your child so she will gain a positive view
of her abilities, especially when she is
tackling a new or difficult challenge,
by saying things like, "You're all right.
I know you can do it.
I'll help if you need me,
but you're doing great!"

156

Help your child see that he is made
for a purpose, just as he is—whether tall
or short, athletic or not, with academic
ability or other talents—and help him
to find that purpose.

157

Build strong "family ties"
by telling your child
the stories of her grandparents'
and parents' courtship and marriage,
joys and difficulties,
using old photos if they are available.
Show her the family tree and the special
branch she fits on.

158

Especially for children with handicaps
or special challenges, give them
"fail-safe" activities that you know
they can succeed in—such as
big black lines to help a visually
impaired child cut paper.

159

Give your child the "gift of availability"
when he wants to talk to you.

160

Play with your child.
Even ten or fifteen minutes of play
with a word game, hide-and-seek,
or outdoor fun builds your relationship.

161

Allow your child to hold an opinion—
even if it is different from yours.
Agree to disagree in a friendly way!

162

Don't overburden your child
with your worries about losing your job,
your difficulties with your spouse
or another relationship,
or financial problems.

163

Let your child make her own
"All About Me" book by getting photos
from babyhood to the present to glue
on pages. She can write a narrative story
under them about the highlights of her life,
illustrate and laminate a cover,
then staple the pages together into a book.

164

Whether your child lets you know it
or not, he craves your affection, loves your
attention, and seeks your guidance.

165

Make your home a learning center
where there are resources and reasons
to read, write, and develop a lifelong
love of learning.

166

Build your "family team"
by including everyone, young and old,
in planning goals and family trips
and solving problems.

167

"Hold a crown a couple of inches
above children's heads and encourage
them to grow into it."
—GEORGE SANCHEZ

168

Show affection to your child
or teen without making her feel
self-conscious: Pat her arm as she
leaves for school and say,
"Love you," give a back rub before bed,
or hold hands during
the dinner table blessing.

169

If you pour concrete for a new patio
or driveway, let your child put in his
handprint, name, and date.

170

Let your child know that her
presence makes a difference:
that you value her input
on matters of importance
to the whole family
by putting into practice
one of her creative ideas to solve
a problem or get a job done.

171

Avoid rescuing your child
out of every difficulty at school
or in sports. Provide loving
support instead.

172

Let your child stay up
a little later one night to have juice
and toast, and ask each
other questions like
"What makes someone a hero?"
"Who is your hero?"
"What can you do to be
a friend to someone?"
"What's the scariest thing
that ever happened to you?"
or other wonderings
of interest to the two of you.

173

Teach your child and his siblings
not to compare themselves
with each other. Instead point out
the unique gifts and abilities
each child has.

174

Share a favorite song with your child
and after listening together,
explain why it is meaningful to you.
Then ask your child to play one
of her favorite songs for you
and afterward talk
about its significance.

175

Have a big family bulletin board
for displaying art work, stories, awards,
notes of encouragement, and photos
of child, parent, and family activities.

176

Don't be afraid to be firm
with your child. Most kids prefer it
because it makes them feel secure.

177

Know your child's friends.
Let them know they are welcome
for dinner and make a place for them
to feel comfortable and play.

178

Help your child develop a hobby
that he enjoys.

179

With your child
get involved in a project
that helps others in need,
such as Habitat for Humanity,
a homeless shelter,
or visiting the elderly in a nursing home.

180
Help your child make Christmas
gifts for friends and family.

181
Serve your child nutritious food,
and teach her about healthy eating
as you cook, cut up vegetables,
and eat out together.

182
Encourage your child to participate
in a sport he likes and to keep at the sport
as he masters the basic skills.

183
Spend an evening or Saturday afternoon
at the library with your child.
Check out books to read together,
an educational game,
or an audiotape to listen to in the car.

184

Take your child to a church
with a dynamic youth program.

185

Talk openly with your child
about the dangers
of drug and alcohol abuse
and what your standards
of behavior are.

186

If your child is struggling
in a school subject,
making a low grade even with effort,
get a tutor for her to help her
fill in the gaps of information
she doesn't understand
and to give her the tools
to succeed.

187

Be visible at your child's school.
Find a way to be involved,
whether it is a once-a-week,
once-a-month, or once-a-semester activity.

188

If you will miss a performance
or big event your child is in at school,
get another parent to videotape it
and watch it together on the weekend.

189

Let your child know he
(and everyone else)
is a "person in process" by saying,
"I like what you are becoming,"
when you see a positive behavior.
"I like how you're becoming a helper
to Mom," or "I love how you're growing
up to be caring toward your friends."

190

Before bedtime,
gather together and share
the "Best Part of the Day."
Each person tells the family what
the favorite or best part of the day was,
while the others listen.
Taking turns, being on "center stage,"
and focusing on the *good* things
that happened are all boosters.

191

"Your child needs your humanness;
be real with him.
This helps him accept
his own humanness,
giving him a model that allows him
to embrace all parts of himself.
Then, he is not alienated
from himself or others."
—DOROTHY CORKILLE BRIGGS

192

Let your child "own" her emotions
without blaming her,
judging, or trying to fix her seemingly
negative feelings.

193

Take time to do creative things
with your child—drawing, painting,
making a collage, or sculpting with clay.
Enjoying art together develops
a bond of understanding between you.

194

Model appropriate coping skills
for dealing with stress, such as talking
instead of acting out frustrations,
finding support, and taking time
for recreation or relaxation.

195

Help your child realize that stress
is normal, problems are a part of life,
and she can learn how to handle it all.

———◆———

196

Have a unique family celebration
for your child on his next birthday.
Arrange pictures of various ages and stages,
and talk about his growth
and accomplishments and the joy
he brings your family.

———◆———

197

Cut out coupons from the Sunday
newspaper with your child and when you
go to the grocery store, ask her to help
find the products and turn in
the coupons. All the money saved is put
in a jar to do something special,
and your child feels she has helped
save the family money.

198

Give your child four compliments
or encouraging words
for every one criticism.

———◆———

199

Show your child how to use
word pictures to express his feelings
(so he won't have to stuff them
or act them out), such as,
"I felt so stressed during the final exams
that it was like vines were
wrapped around my neck,"
or "I was so excited about the first
soccer game it was like I was a balloon
about to pop."

———◆———

200

Build an atmosphere of safety and security
at home for your child.

201

Encourage your child to help other children, especially those who have newly moved to the school or are physically challenged.

202

Take the time to watch your kindergarten or early elementary child go through her backpack each day after school to "ooh" and "aah" over her hard work and drawings.

203

When visiting a grandparent or great aunt in a nursing home, have your child bring something for the other residents in the wing such as candy, a picture he drew, cookies he helped make, and greet each one.

204

Aim for a parenting style in which you are
in control but listen to your child,
are nurturing, affectionate,
and communicative.

205

Touch has the positive power of helping
a child feel cared for, loved, and secure.

206

Encourage your child to tell you what she
likes and dislikes and why:
everything from what is served for dinner
to her favorite cartoon and book.

207

All children need limits
to feel secure and safe.

208

Help your child be aware
of his negative self-talk—"I messed up
in math; I'm so dumb,"
"I can't do anything"—and replace it
with constructive thoughts—"I didn't
make the grade I wanted
on the math test,
but next time I'll get extra help."

209

Start a "Secret Samaritan" game.
Encourage each person
to do good deeds
for others anonymously.
The thoughtful projects can be
simple or elaborate:
polish Dad's shoes while he's at work,
leave Mom a note and flower
in the kitchen,
rake a neighbor's leaves.

210

Have a "Family Night" once a week.
Everyone has input
on what you do together:
go to a movie or museum,
play games and eat popcorn,
dine at a favorite restaurant.

———◆———

211

Share with your kids,
"Mom (or Dad)
hasn't been to school
in a long time.
Can you tell me something
each day that you have found out
to help me keep learning?"
Then on the way home
from school or at dinner
each child talks about
the brand-new fact or discovery.

212

When you can, attend your
child's sports or other practices
to let her know the drills
and hard work she put in
are important to you.

213

Limit television watching;
pick a few high-quality programs
he can watch each week,
thereby increasing
your child's creativity
and resourcefulness.

214

Record an audio or videotape
of your child playing an instrument,
reading a story, or singing a song.

215

Give your child a monogrammed or
personalized towel, pillowcase, or other gift.

216

Attend your child's Open House night
and parent-teacher conferences.

217

Model the positive habit
of making, cultivating,
and keeping friendships.

218

Be there at your child's
milestones—confirmation or baptism,
graduation from kindergarten,
middle school, and high school—
and celebrate them together.

219

If your child regularly comes
home from school depressed or begins
to dread going, confer with your child
and the teacher about the problem
and come up with a plan of action.

220

Wear the necklace or tie your child
gave you for your birthday;
use the goofy mug or hang up
the plaque she picked out.

221

Take a course or work on a new skill.
Let your child see you enjoying
your own curiosity and learning
from new experiences.

222

Teach your child to knit or crochet,
do woodworking or another skill
you have mastered.

———◆———

223

Give your child your phone number
at work and let him know he can call you.

———◆———

224

Offer (but don't force)
your assistance when your child
has to memorize—such as
orally practicing Spanish vocabulary
words or going over her speech
to run for Student Council.

225

Keep academics in proper perspective,
and help your child maintain a balance
between school work and other areas
important to his growth: emotional,
intellectual, physical, and spiritual.

226

Let your child know that you
are committed to her for life:
"I love you and will be here for you,
no matter what happens."

227

Teach your child it is okay
to say no when asked by a peer
or an adult to use alcohol or drugs.
Be a role model as he sees you say no to
alcoholic beverages,
second or third helpings of food,
and purchases outside your budget.

228

Help your child cope
with her anger, so she doesn't
have to fear you'll disapprove of
or reject her when she's angry.
Putting it into words
and identifying the source
of the anger helps.

229

As a family, be focused more
on *giving* than on *getting*.

230

At Thanksgiving,
suggest that your child write
a note of appreciation
to his teachers for all the effort they
put into his education.

231

Find a group for your child
to become involved with to learn
cooperation, teamwork, and perhaps
leadership skills: Boy Scouts, Girl Scouts
or Campfire Girls, 4-H Clubs,
a band or orchestra,
or youth group at church.

232

Make a big calendar
together and mark events,
holidays, school activities,
and family plans to look forward to.

233

Have a "Classic Movie Night."
Rent an old movie, snuggle up,
and watch together.
Afterward, talk about the characters
you and your child most
identified with and why.

234

Learn about child development
so you will know what your child
is capable of at every age
and what you can expect
mentally, physically,
and emotionally.
You'll save yourself and your child
much frustration!

235

Give your young child verbal cues
that will help her transition
from one place or one activity
to another. (*Examples:* "In ten minutes
we'll leave for school,"
"Start wrapping up your playing,"
or "There's twenty minutes
until bedtime.")

236

Begin to give your three-year-old
choices (a two-year-old has
a harder time with choices):
which book to read,
Curious George
or *Richard Scarry*,
to draw or fingerpaint at art time, etc.

237

"Think of child development as a clock.
Some clocks run fast; some clocks run
slow. Some take awhile to wind up
and then sprint very quickly."
—ANN BENJAMIN

238

Sit down and play a game of cards
with your child.

239

Make a family Christmas album
in which you put a few photos
from each parent's
and your children's first Christmases,
photos from each holiday season,
of guests and visitors,
and of performances
your child is in.

240

Children need love the most
when they deserve it the least.

241

Respect your child's
teachers and principal and insist
he do the same.

242

Talk to your child about the future,
about interesting careers,
and help her to think about what
she'd like to be and do.

243

Don't be afraid to say "no" to your child.

244

If your child wants to tackle a job
that seems too big for him,
let him try it, and you will often
be pleasantly surprised!

245

"A child's feelings of personal worth
will never be greater than the worth
her family finds in her."
—ELAINE MCEWAN

246

Provide a strong support
network for your child
with a caring neighbor, teacher,
close family friend, or relative.
Having additional adults
in your child's life
(especially in times of crisis
or extra stress) contributes much
to emotional stability.

247

As author John Trent says,
turn "contact points" into
"caring points" as his mother did,
meeting him and his siblings
with bright eyes as glad
to see them as if they were
long-lost friends.

248
Let your child see that her education
is important to you.

249
Build a positive relationship
with your child's teacher.

250
"Far too often, we spend most of our time
pulling weeds in the garden of our children's
lives, instead of fertilizing the flowers."
—KEN DAVIS

251
Find a mentor for your child in his field
of interest. If it's medicine, match him
with a doctor; if it's design, see if he can
help a graphic artist on Saturdays.

252

Children develop self-confidence
through handling struggles
and overcoming them.

253

Believe in yourself
and your worth as a parent.
Know that you have valuable things
to pass on, many skills, and much love
to give to your child.

254

Play a memory game
with your child and show her
your own secrets to remembering
certain important information.

255

Build confidence in your parenting
and gain skills by attending
a parents' support group
at your church or community center.

256

Together make a tree house
or backyard fort and let your child
hammer and help build it.

257

Avoid overreacting or being
very upset when your child
loses a competition or fails
in some endeavor,
and help him learn
to persevere.

258

The average child asks 500,000
questions by the age of fifteen.
Take advantage of these
"teachable moments" by
showing interest
and enthusiasm about your
child's questions.

259

Keep a photo of your child
in your billfold and on your desk
or work center.

260

Avoid threatening your child.

261

"An ounce of praise can
accomplish more
than a ton of faultfinding.
And, if one looks for it,
something worthy of praise
can be found in every child."
—JOHN DRESCHER

262

Know what humiliates your child
in front of her friends and avoid doing it.

263

Begin making a tape recording
of your child's voice,
talking about what he's currently doing
and interested in.
Add to it once each year.
It's great to play it back later
when he's older.

264

Know what "de-stresses"
your child best
on a stressful day—is it physical activity,
a listening ear, quiet music,
a nutritious snack,
a walk around the block?

265

As Dr. James Dobson says,
give your child independence
and responsibility in gradual steps,
so that when she is beyond
your control (i.e., in college)
she will no longer need it:
Let a preteen pick her own outfits,
a fifteen-year-old manage
her own clothing budget,
and a seventeen-year-old
save summer salary
for car insurance.

266
Find a balance between rigidity
and permissiveness
as you parent your child.

———◆———

267
Help your child or teen with problem
solving, but don't take over his problem;
talk about available help and the information
he needs to deal with his mistakes
and problems.

———◆———

268
When your child makes a mistake,
make sure imposed penalties
or consequences are appropriate
for the mistake.
If a teen is an hour late from her Friday-
night date, subtracting one hour
from her Saturday-night curfew
is more realistic
than grounding her for a month.

269

Form links with other parents at school
to compare notes on what the kids
do together after school and on weekends,
and work together to provide
direction for them.

270

When your child feels needed
by the family
it's a terrific self-esteem builder.
When you need help,
entrust jobs to your child,
and acknowledge work well done.

271

Give your child one-to-one
nuggets of your time.
Go out for an ice cream cone and talk,
wash the car together, bird watch,
or walk the mall.

272

When your child has
an audition or competition
he is nervous about, encourage him
to envision himself doing
exactly what he needs to do
and doing it right—whether that
is a song, a cheer,
or a wrestling move.
Picturing success builds confidence.

273

When your child practices
her instrument,
sit in the room now and then
to hear her play.
Then say something positive
and specific about a piece played
or technique improved.

274

When your child doesn't make
the team or doesn't succeed
at an important audition,
let him experience his sad feelings;
then lovingly reassure him
of his importance
in the family regardless
of the outcome.

———◆———

275

"Children are more likely
to be achievers if their parents
join together to give
the same clear and positive
message about school effort
and expectations."
—SYLVIA RIMM

276

Focus high-energy children
by finding positive active involvement
for them.

277

Point out your child's positive character
traits when you see them in action,
such as compassion,
effort, kindness, service,
or diligence.

278

When your child reads a novel
assigned in the classroom,
get a paperback of the book
and read it yourself to open up
some fine discussion.

279

Plan, shop for, and prepare a meal together from a different ethnic menu than you are used to.

280

When parents or other adults talk together about their kids' shortcomings with them in earshot, negative traits are reinforced: "Molly's room is always a wreck; she's the messiest child we have," or "Ben is just not trying in math, and I'm giving up helping him." Instead, let them overhear you discussing a good report about each child.

281

Model hard work and achievement
before your child,
and avoid complaining
about your job.

282

Let your child know you trust her
to keep her promises
and to tell you the truth.

283

Request the right to inspect your child's
permanent school records each year
and to have deleted from the file
any disparaging comments
that would damage
his progress in school.

284

Do not allow your child to be
negatively labeled at school.
When children are branded
with labels they often become
self-fulfilling prophecies;
better to get your child the help
and modifications needed
for learning without a label.

285

Avoid laughing at your child or teenager
when she makes a mistake
or does something foolish.

286

Fair and reasonable rules at home
are strong evidence
of love and caring.

287

Have a potluck supper
in your home,
and invite a few families
who have children
the same age as your child
or a best friend or two
and their families.

288

Share with the teacher some
of your child's interests
and strengths
and ask if there could be a way
for him to connect
his interest with the subjects
being studied.

289

Help your child develop strength
and coordination in her body
and confidence in moving by regular
exercise, playing physically challenging
games, and having outdoor play.

290

Give your child time for a social life
and building relationships with friends.

291

Don't force your child
to dress 180 degrees differently
than all the other children.
Cooperate together on wise shopping
and let your child help
find good buys on clothing
and shoes.

292

Help your child see situations
from another person's point of view
to build a sense of empathy.

293

Fill your child's reservoir
with encouragement, love, acceptance,
and understanding.

294

Keep your promises.

295

When your child asks a question,
encourage him to find the answer
by asking, "How do you think
we can find out?"

296

Help your child
make a time capsule
to open on a future birthday
or New Year.
In a shoebox
she can put photos,
laminated newspaper headlines,
souvenirs, and mementoes.
Date the box,
seal it, and hide it
in a safe place.

297

At the end of the year, make a family
poster depicting the best memories
and events. Get a large piece
of posterboard and let each person either
cut out pictures and words
from magazines or draw a picture
of the most favorite time together.

298

Buy a can of breadstick dough
and have your child twist and form
the dough into the letters
of his name.
Brush the tops
with butter, bake, and eat.

299

When you travel, send your child
a postcard with a special message
from each place you visit.

300

Home should be the place
where young people
can bring their problems, hurts,
and disappointments and be sure
of finding understanding, acceptance,
and security.

301

Encourage your child to make gift
certificates to give as presents
to family members
on Christmas or birthdays.
A certificate good for a service
(one week of setting the table
or two breakfasts in bed)
is a wonderful gift.

302

"Expect the best from your kids—
then rejoice with whatever you get."
—KEN DAVIS

303

Give your child the opportunity to reach
out and help others with whatever
resources you have: giving toys
and outgrown clothes to a youth shelter,
buying baby supplies
for an infant crisis center.

304

Be a treasure hunter
and look for the gold in your child.

305

Some of the best qualities of adults
are "irritating" in kids or seem negative
to parents—an argumentative child may
have analytical gifts, a bossy child
administrative potential and the natural
ability to run a major company.

306

At the end of the school year, ask,
"What would you *most* like to do
this summer?"
Get out a big piece of butcher paper
and let each family member cut out
and glue on magazine pictures of things
he or she looks forward to.
Then try to do as many as possible.

307

Make sure your child learns to read *well*.
If she has some initial difficulties,
get a tutor or help her yourself.

308

Balance discipline with lots of love
and affection.

309

Choose stories and books
that have the protagonist
dealing with
the same problems
your child is facing.
By identifying with the character
and how he dealt with struggles,
your child is helped to face
his own problems.

310

"When a teen pushes parents away
in the journey toward independence,
parents often respond by distancing
themselves. Think of the parent/teen
relationship as two people at opposite
ends of the same rope, each tugging.
If you both keep tugging while also
negotiating, you get closer to the middle.
But if you let go of the rope,
your child falls down completely,
and may be in trouble."
—ADELE FABER

311

Teach your child self-restraint
by not fulfilling every demand
immediately. Encourage her to think
for twenty-four hours
before she buys an item,
save for something big she wants
(and go halves with her), and set goals
and work toward them on a daily basis.

312

Stop and smell the roses.
Enjoy life with your child today.

313

Forgive your child
when he has disappointed you,
hurt you, or failed.
The inability to forgive
has a damaging effect
on the family and keeps a parent
focused on the
child's weaknesses.

314

Show real, visible trust
in your child.
Let her know you believe in her
and are counting on her
to do the right thing.

315
Get your child
his own library card
and encourage frequent use.

316
After an improved test score,
take your child out
for pizza just like you would
after a winning soccer game.

317
Be interested in content,
what your child
is learning in each course,
not just in the grade.

318

Prepare your child for the somewhat
rough waters of adolescence
when her self-image may be fragile
and physical and social changes occur.
Read a book together
on preparing for adolescence.

319

Have a "sticky tape walk" with your child
in which you place masking tape around
his wrists with the sticky side out.
In autumn, look for signs of fall and put
those on the tape. When you get home,
make a collage of what you have found.

320

Have adult friends and family members
over to your home who can model healthy
self-confidence and show your child
how to take life head-on.

321

Establish traditions
and make memories for your child.
As author Edith Schaeffer says,
"Memories ought to be planned,
chosen, memories ought to be
put in the budget,
memories ought to be recognized
and given the proper amount of time,
memories ought to be protected,
memories ought not to be wasted,
and memories ought
to be passed down
to the next generation."

322

Affirm your child's present
accomplishment,
whether that is making her bed well,
learning to read,
or tying her shoes.

323

Avoid redoing things your child
has done: remaking the bed,
re-ironing the shirt,
or vacuuming the carpet
over again to get it more "perfect."

324

At a family reunion,
give your child a disposable camera,
a tape recorder with blank tape,
and a short list of questions
to ask relatives
to reminisce about their past.

325

Given our culture,
if your child is not physically attractive,
it is even more important
to help him develop a special talent
that can bring him recognition.

326

All children have talent, giftedness,
and promise in some area,
and patient support from parents
can help talents bloom.

327

If your child understands her own
learning style and how to work with it,
she will be more motivated and confident
at school.

328

Don't force your shy child
to be outgoing or into situations
he is uncomfortable with.
Provide chances to develop
his interests and talk
about them one-on-one.

329

If you struggle with feelings
of low self-worth,
you are likely to take your child's
disobedience as rejection of you.
Work on developing
a healthy perspective of yourself
and you can better
help your child grow in self-worth.

330

One of the best opportunities to affirm
your support of your child
is when the pain of a failure
has shaken her world.
This is a good time to say,
"I know you're disappointed.
On other days, you'll have
other chances.
You're always special
and important to me."

331

Help your child put a problem
into words and then brainstorm aloud
about various ways to solve it.

332

Show your child how to receive
a compliment by taking turns
praising each person
in the family for something
he or she is doing. If your child
looks down and ignores
a compliment, later you could say,
"It would be nice
if you acknowledged me
when I compliment you.
Smiling or saying thanks
is one way to do it."

333

When you carpool to and from school
and sports practices with your child
and others, use your time together
and make it fun—tell a story
with continuing episodes, play word
or license plate games,
or sing along to a tape.

334

If your family moves to a different city,
smooth the transition by inviting a child
and parent from the new neighborhood
over, taking an early visit to the school,
keeping up family rituals, and sightseeing.

335

Make sure your child knows
how to call 911 and which neighbor
to call in case he has a need
or emergency when you are not home.

336

Instead of going "all out"
for a once-a-month outing
with your child,
trying to make up for lost time,
fill the little pockets of time
you have each day
with loving, fun moments
spent together.

337

As Dr. James Dobson says,
"Save some energy for the teenage years,
because you are going to need it!"
Learn to pace yourself, find enjoyable ways
to refuel by having lunch with a friend,
coop-babysitting with other parents,
and building in an "R and R"
(rest and read) time
for your kids each day.

338

Arrange your home so that baby or toddler can explore her environment safely and without excessive restriction.

339

Start a family newsletter and distribute to extended family members (aunts, uncles, college cousins, grandparents). It's a great place to share news, accomplishments, graduations, and travels, of the youngest to the oldest, and gives children wonderful role models "across the miles."

340

If you are disappointed because your child isn't naturally athletic, scholastic, or relational, adjust your expectations to more realistic ones. Accept his weaknesses. Celebrate who he is now and focus on his strengths.

341

As much as possible,
be consistent in discipline.
When discipline is inconsistent,
your child is never quite sure
what behavior is expected.

342

Unplug the television for a week
and get out games, collections, photo
albums to add pictures to, art supplies
to create with, and enjoy the chance
to talk together.

343

Tape record with your voice
your child's favorite stories and books
to play on her tape recorder when you
travel as a family
or go away on business.

344

Instead of intervening and trying
to settle every sibling dispute,
close your ears to tattling
and encourage them
to work out conflicts.

345

Read your child the biographies
of great people who contributed much
to our society or to their times.

346

Gather clues from teacher conferences,
report cards, and observation to learn
your child's weaknesses
that are holding him back,
and get the support and help needed,
such as eyeglasses for poor vision,
speech therapy, or a reading tutor.

347

Show your child how to manage
her time with a daily notebook calendar
to list assignments, a weekly "To Do" list,
and a code to prioritize the most
important to least important duties.

348

When you tutor your own child in math
or another subject, sit side by side,
explain directions slowly with visual aids
or hands-on materials, and be
encouraging rather than negative,
saying, "You're getting close,"
instead of "You're wrong."

349

Whenever you get the chance,
model sportsmanship for your child,
taking defeat in stride, congratulating
winners, and encourage your child to do
the same in his competitions.

350

Read stories and books
to your child in which the characters
portray the values and attitudes
you want your child to embrace.

351

Give your child opportunities
to be alone and learn to enjoy
the quiet of his room,
listening to his own music,
writing in a journal, or making things.

352

Find out what units are being taught
in history and science,
and get videos and books
to supplement.

353

Before your family moves,
provide your child
with an address book
to collect friends' addresses
and phone numbers,
and help her make postcards
with your new address to hand out.
Keeping in touch with old friends
provides a sense of roots
and connection.

354

If your child has special academic needs,
don't wait for a new teacher
to discover them. Meet and discuss
what modifications can be made
to help him succeed
and learn in the classroom.

355

Prepare your child for what is going
to happen, especially if she is young
or struggles with attention problems,
and her behavior will be better:
"The Smiths are coming for dinner
tonight," "In thirty minutes we leave
for the band concert."

356

Keep your child's curiosity alive
by doing kitchen and backyard
science experiments, getting an ant farm,
or catching fireflies.

357

Show your child how to ask for help
from the librarian, postal delivery person,
or other people in your daily life.
Then role-play his asking for help
from the teacher, a store clerk, etc.

358

If your child tries hard in school
and still struggles, share with her
that Winston Churchill, Pearl Buck,
Ray Kroc (founder of McDonald's),
Albert Einstein, Eleanor Roosevelt,
and many other outstanding
people had trouble in school
and still succeeded in life and made
great contributions.

359

If your child brings home
a disappointing report card,
keep the ball in his court
by asking questions like,
"How do you feel about your grades?"
"Do you want to bring up your marks
in a subject, and how can we help?"
"Can you think of any changes
to make in your studying?"

360

Share with your child the reasons
you are grateful and happy
to be her parent.

361

Get your child an alarm clock
and let him be responsible for setting it
at night, getting up and dressed
for school at the proper time.

362

Hold regular "Family Forums,"
meetings to discuss the calendar
and activities for the next week,
chores to delegate,
complaints, and solutions to problems.
Finish the meeting with a simple dessert
and by pointing out the strengths
of each family member.

363

"Make a 'Storytelling Stocking' for your child. Sew twenty-four ribbons to a Christmas stocking, and put twenty-four special items inside: the bootie Grandma knitted for her, her first comb, a camp ribbon, etc. Each day in December, let her pick an item, tie it to the front of the stocking, and tell her the story behind it. As she grows, she tells the stories (items inside can be added or changed)."

—POSY LOUGH

364

Get an album to collect your child's birthday cards from babyhood up, and add to it each year. On a rainy day or when he is ill, bring out the card album, read the messages, and talk about the givers and how each one is connected to the family.

365

Tell your child
you love her every single night
and though you scold her
make sure you hold her and tell her—
"Everything's all right!
Tomorrow's looking bright!"

Author

Cheri Fuller is an experienced educator who has taught at every level from elementary to college. She is the author of six previous books and numerous articles in *Family Circle, CHILD, Focus on the Family*, and others. She has also appeared on many television and radio programs, and is a popular speaker to parent groups and teacher seminars. She and her husband, Holmes, live in Oklahoma City with their three children.

Other books by Cheri Fuller, also available from Piñon Press: *Unlocking Your Child's Learning Potential, 365 Ways to Help Your Child Learn and Achieve*, and *365 Ways to Develop Your Child's Values*.

703281 2657